P9-DUX-033

Darrell Buehl,
Please do your part to honor and
support America's Disabled Veterans,
and make a donation today to the
Disabled Veterans National Foundation
by going to www.dvnf.org or sending
your gift to: Disabled Veterans National
Foundation, PO Box 96648, Washington, D.C.
20090-6648.

　　　　　　　　　Thanks,
G310905　　　　　Joe
46821LN

A Message

from DVNF Chief Executive Officer, Joe VanFonda

Dear Friend,

As I reflect on the beauty and bounty of this land, awe strikes my heart. When the first pilgrims touched the eastern shore of this place we call America, they never imagined the myriad wonders it would reveal! What a treasure – a vast expanse as varied as those who would one day people it … brimming with lush forests, majestic mountains, rivers, deserts, prairies, plains, seascapes and lakeshores.

Through our history, our cathedral has been a vast and ever-changing sky, our altar the great mountains. In the shadow of such natural wonders – so beautifully showcased in this collectible book – generations toiled to make America what it is today. Through sweat and tears and vision and virtue, America grew to become the greatest country in the world, freedom's powerful champion.

From the start, there were those who would try to destroy freedom, who would steal the precious bounty of this great land. They were defeated by patriots who put country above self to protect us, sacrificing their blood and their health to keep our land and our people safe and free.

Today another generation has taken up the cause of liberty and justice in the world. You won't find their faces in the pages of this book, yet their sacrifice preserves these wonderful places. Because Americans in uniform put their lives on the line, you and I can rest easy, can walk safely down our streets, can marvel at autumn leaves and fragrant spring flowers.

These pages are devoted to America's disabled veterans, who have long preserved our nation and our way of life. But this book also pays homage to people like you, who care for the millions of heroes wounded in our defense.

With Humble Gratitude,

Joseph VanFonda
USMC Sergeant Major Retired
DVNF Chief Executive Officer

Oh, say...

can you see

by the dawn's

early light

What so proudly

we hailed

at the twilight's

last gleaming

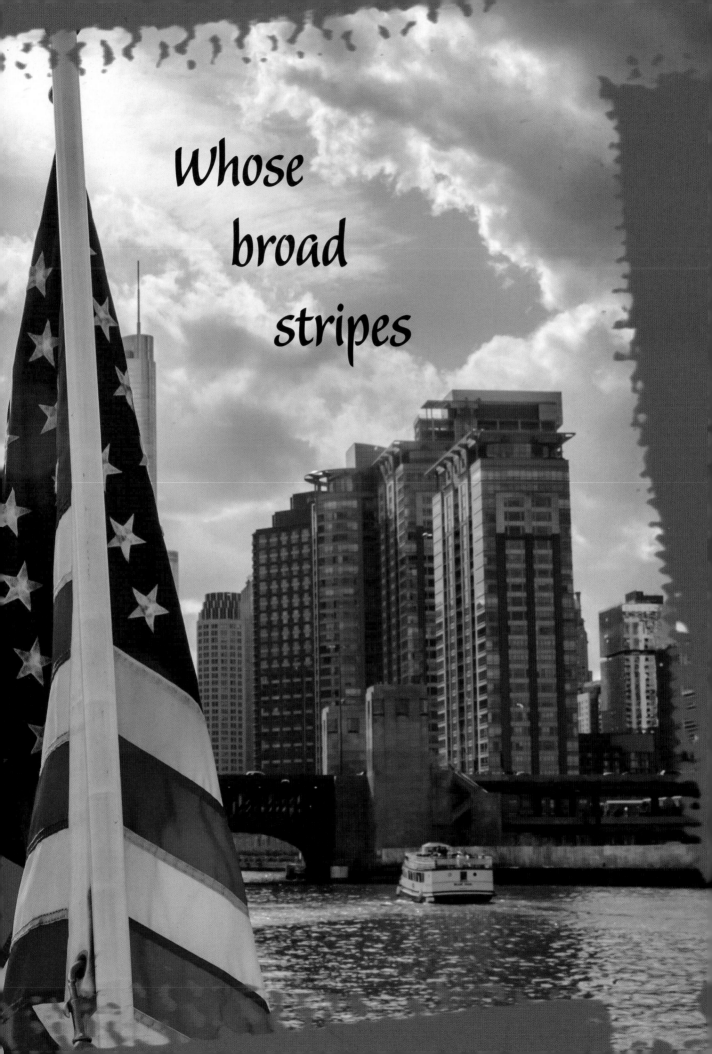

Whose
broad
stripes

and bright stars

O'er the ramparts we watched

Bless
erica

were so
gallantly
streaming

And
the rocket's
red glare

the bombs bursting

in air

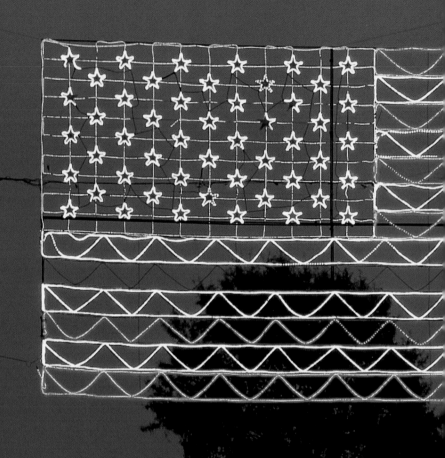

Gave proof through the night

that our flag

was still there

Oh, say

does that

star-spangled banner

yet wave

O'er the land
    of the free

and
the
home

of the brave?